WALSALL
IN LIVING MEMORY

BRITAIN IN OLD PHOTOGRAPHS

WALSALL

IN LIVING MEMORY

DAVID F. VODDEN

SUTTON PUBLISHING

Sutton Publishing Limited
Phoenix Mill · Thrupp · Stroud
Gloucestershire · GL5 2BU

First published 2006

Title-page photograph: Savoy Cinema, 1946.
(*D.F. Vodden Collection*)

British Library Cataloguing in Publication Data
A catalogue record for this book is available from the
British Library.

ISBN 0-7509-4322-X

Typeset in 10.5/13.5pt Photina.
Typesetting and origination by
Sutton Publishing Limited.
Printed and bound in England by
J.H. Haynes & Co. Ltd, Sparkford.

THE BLACK COUNTRY SOCIETY

The Black Country Society is proud to be associated with **Sutton Publishing** of Stroud. In 1994 the society was invited by Sutton Publishing to collaborate in what has proved to be a highly successful publishing partnership, namely the extension of the **Britain in Old Photographs** series into the Black Country. In this joint venture the Black Country Society has played an important role in establishing and developing a major contribution to the region's photographic archives by encouraging society members to compile books of photographs of the area or town in which they live.

The first book in the Black Country series was *Wednesbury in Old Photographs* by Ian Bott, launched by Lord Archer of Sandwell in November 1994. Since then almost 70 Black Country titles have been published. The total number of photographs contained in these books is in excess of 13,000, suggesting that the whole collection is probably the largest regional photographic survey of its type in any part of the country to date.

This voluntary society was founded in 1967 as a reaction to the trends of the late 1950s and early '60s. This was a time when the reorganisation of local government was seen as a threat to the identity of individual communities and when, in the name of progress and modernisation, the industrial heritage of the Black Country was in danger of being swept away.

The general aims of the society are to stimulate interest in the past, present and future of the Black Country, and to secure at regional and national levels an accurate understanding and portrayal of what constitutes the Black Country and, wherever possible, to encourage and facilitate the preservation of the Black Country's heritage.

The society, which now has over 2,500 members worldwide, organises a yearly programme of activities. There are six venues in the Black Country where evening meetings are held on a monthly basis from September to April. In the summer months, there are fortnightly guided evening walks in the Black Country and its green borderland, and there is also a full programme of excursions further afield by car. Details of all these activities are to be found on the society's website, **www.blackcountrysociety.co.uk**, and in *The Blackcountryman*, the quarterly magazine that is distributed to all members.

PO Box 71 · Kingswinford · West Midlands DY6 9YN

CONTENTS

ACKNOWLEDGEMENTS

I would like to thank the following people for their help and encouragement, and for the use of old photographs and supporting information published in this book: Mrs Margaret Anderson, Mr and Mrs Ken Baldwin, the late Mr John Barratt, the late Mr Jack Booth, Mr Bob Brevitt, Mr D. Burwell, the late Mr Horace Cross, Mrs Kath Evans, Mr David Farrell, Mr and Mrs Brian Felgate, Dr Leslie Fox, Mrs Mary Fryer, Mrs Eileen Goodwin, Mr Brian Griffiths, Mr John Griffiths, Mr Jack Haddock, Mr Peter Hall, Mr Steve Hanson, Mr John Harper, Mr Terry Harrison, Mr and Mrs John Hateley, Mr Martin Hateley, Mrs Jane Highfield, Mr Tony Highfield, Mr Stan Hill, Mrs Norma Hilton, the late Dr Charles Hollingsworth, Mr Phil Holmes, Mr John Hubble, Mr Cliff Hubbold, Mrs Pixie Jenkins (née Tibbits), Mrs Shirley Lacey, Mr Clem Lewis, Mr Chris Madeley, Mr and Mrs Jim McBride, Mr Roy Meller, Mr Ted Moorman (former Mayor), Mrs Rita Mycock (née Sims), Cllr E.W. Newman (former Mayor), Mr Jack Page, Mr Don Payne, Mr John Pearson, Mr Roger Pinson, Mr and Mrs Everitt Plater, Mr Wilf Price, Mr Roy Spencer, Mr Roy Taylor, Dr Stephen Taylor, Mr and Mrs Richard Vodden, Mr Gordon Whiston, Mr David Wilkins (First House Photography), Mr Stuart Williams, Mrs Pam Winton, Mr Craig Winyard (*Walsall Observer*, now *Walsall Advertiser*) and Mr Phil Wood (former Mayor).

INTRODUCTION

The Allied triumph over Hitler's Germany ensured the freedom we enjoy today. Yet despite the poppies, the postwar memorials and the annual services of remembrance, the contributions made to that victory by a wide variety of Britons are all too easily forgotten.

Michael Smith, *Station X*,
London, Channel 4 Books, 1998

The Second World War affected Walsall in many ways. There were enemy air raids, men and women left home to serve in the forces, while others did war work in Civil Defence or worked long hours in munitions factories or coal mines.

The day after war broke out, on 4 September 1939, 340 Walsall children were evacuated to Brewood and Penkridge. There were also periods of severe weather, commencing in January–February 1940 with the 'hardest winter in living memory'. In October German bombers dropped flares on the municipal golf course (see David F. Vodden, *Our Black Country*, Stroud, Sutton Publishing, 2003, p. 92).

The late John Barratt remembered 4 June 1941, when HE bombs landed on the golf course badly damaging his family home. The next day it rained to add further misery, most of the tiles having been blown off the roof. Days later, he and young *Walsall Times* reporter Clem Lewis recalled bombs being dropped on William Bates's Hospital Street factory, killing eight firewatchers.

On Armistice Day 1940, 19-year-old Norman Bailey became another casualty – struck by shrapnel from an AA shell. At 3.30 p.m. that same day, a Junkers 88 bombed the Corporation Gas Works in Pleck, as a result of which Noel Hateley was awarded the George Medal for bravery, an award instituted only in September of the same year by King George VI. Those involved were given a civic reception by the Mayor, Alderman Cliff Tibbits. Clem Lewis further recalled the Bridgwood family, including their seven children, had just returned to their house in Blakenall after the all-clear siren, when a late direct hit destroyed their Anderson shelter in which they had been hiding, in October 1940. Fortunately for this area, the Germans turned their attention to the so-called Baedeker Raids, commencing three days after bombing Pleck Gasworks, with the infamous Coventry air raid.

Many firms both large and small became munitions factories, made uniforms (see also Vodden, *Our Black Country*, pp. 51, 95) or even assembled gas masks, as at Crabtrees.

During 1943 the first US troops were stationed in the area, principally at Whittington Barracks, Lichfield. Good relations with them were celebrated in February 1945.

When VE day arrived, heralded for weeks as V Day, there were street parties and general rejoicing (see also Vodden, *Our Black Country*, pp. 96–7). Some servicemen and women, such as David Partridge, were in the 'Forgotten Army', continuing to fight the Japanese until 15 August 1945.

Menfolk eventually came back from the various fronts and the town, despite bad winters, began to undergo changes such as the clearing of Church Hill and, towards the end of the 1960s, the rebuilding of Old Square and High Street (see also Vodden, David F., *Walsall Revisited*, Stroud, Sutton Publishing, 1997, pp. 12–15).

The Town Plan, devised in 1945, did not, however, meet with the approval of architect Rob Madeley who made alternative, but unadopted, proposals.

Walsall soon did well for royal visits. The Queen, as Princess Elizabeth, came to Crabtrees (see also Vodden, *Walsall Revisited*, pp. 88–91) and was closely followed by Princess Margaret, who completed a different full programme on 1 May 1951 (see also pp. 49–50 and 96). The same year, the Festival of Britain was celebrated in fine style (see also Vodden, *Our Black Country*, p. 67).

Having carried out duties such as being despatch riders for the fire service during the war, the Scout movement continued to thrive in the decades that followed. Pictures and information have been mostly obtained from the 3rd Walsall Sea Scouts and the 16th St Matthew's Own Troop. While the Sea Scouts kept a fine set of leather-bound logbooks, the St Matthew's records are largely culled from the extensive archive left by Scout Commissioner, Alf (Tiny) Felgate, all of which reflect lively activity and considerable achievement. Many pictured here have now become prominent people in the town.

The 1960s also saw the building of leading educational establishments, with the Technical College, Queen Mary's Grammar School and the West Midlands College being completed successfully despite the very severe winter of 1962/3. That year the frozen Arboretum lake provided opportunity for skating, tobogganing and ice hockey for a few months.

The redevelopment of Digbeth and the Old Square (see also David F. Vodden, *Walsall Past and Present*, Stroud, Sutton Publishing, 1999, pp. 26–36) has been followed by the transformation of High Street, The Bridge (Civic Square), a new bus station and Park Street, with the addition of the Walsall New Art Gallery and Gallery Square leading to Wolverhampton Street and Crown Wharf.

Most recently, Leicester Street, Darwall Street and Tower Street have been largely pedestrianised to provide a Civic Quarter and a new setting for the municipal buildings.

In the not-too-distant future, Walsall will have a new Asda, a new technical college and a new Tesco, with an improved Littleton Street to ease through traffic. The relatively new Woolworths may go to make room for a Metro tram terminus and to provide access to Crown Wharf in Wolverhampton Street.

Since the outbreak of war, Walsall has seen many changes; manufacturing industry has been replaced by service industries and the street scene has been, and continues to be, transformed into a town centre very different to that of 1939.

David F. Vodden
September 2006

1

Walsall from the Air

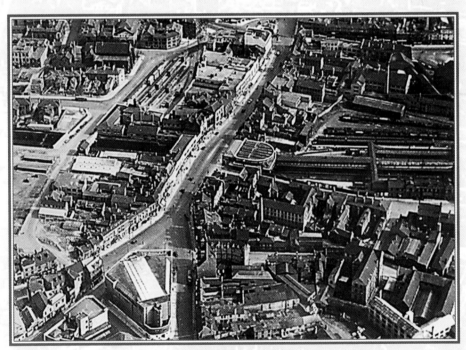

West of Park Street, 1940s. (*D.F. Vodden Collection*)

Walsall in 1996 is photographed from above St Matthew's Church and looks down High Street, over the Overstrand, across The Bridge and up the brick-paved Part Street. (*Courtesy First House Photography*)

Compare this view of Walsall taken in 1999 with that taken in 1996. The new bus station is nearing completion and Woolworths is finished. (*Courtesy First House Photography*)

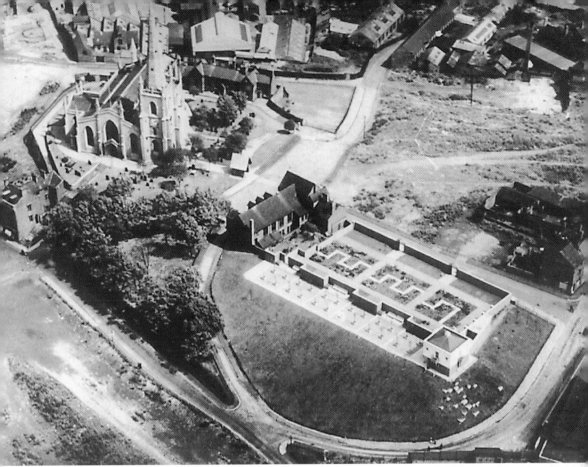

St Matthew's Parish Church in 1950, showing how the surrounding area had been cleared and landscaped soon after the war. (*D.F. Vodden Collection*)

Opposite: Walsall, 2001. (*Courtesy D. Wilkins, First House Photography*)

St Matthew's Parish
Church in the 1970s.
(*D.F. Vodden*)

Walsall, 1996.
(*Courtesy First House
Photography*)

2

The Second World War

Pleck Gasworks from the air, 1949. Number 2 gasholder had received a direct hit in 1940 and was not used again, while a second bomb just missed the Retort House on the right. Noel Hateley lived on site in the house top right. The works were finally demolished in August 1975. (*John Griffiths Collection*)

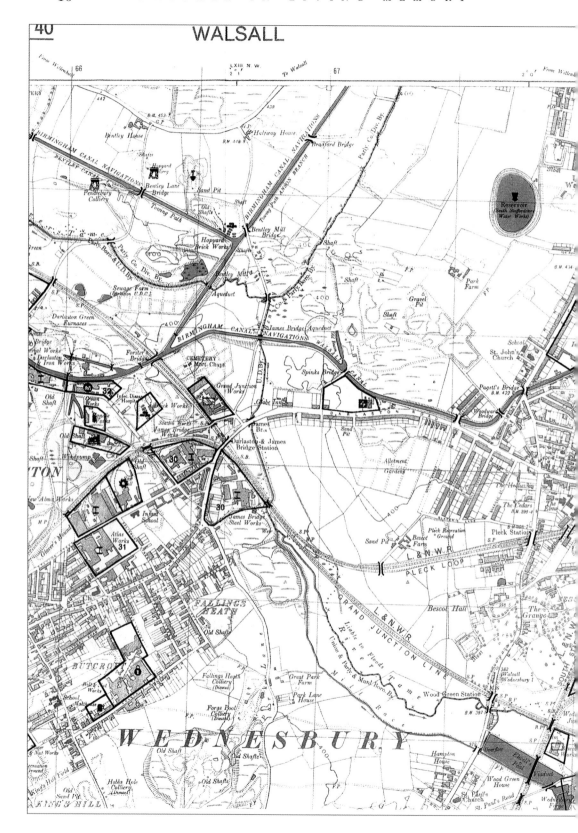

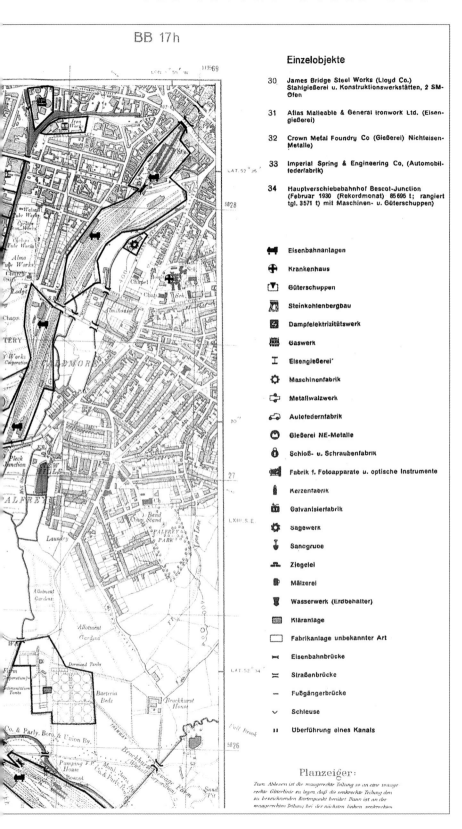

BB 17h

Einzelobjekte

30 James Bridge Steel Works (Lloyd Co.) Stahlgießerei u. Konstruktionswerkstätten, 2 SM-Öfen

31 Atlas Malleable & General Ironwork Ltd. (Eisengießerei)

32 Crown Metal Foundry Co (Gießerei) Nichteisen-Metalle)

33 Imperial Spring & Engineering Co, (Automobilfederfabrik)

34 Hauptverschiebebahnhof Bescot-Junction (Februar 1930 (Rekordmonat) 85 695 t; rangiert tgl. 3571 t) mit Maschinen- u. Güterschuppen)

Eisenbahnanlagen

Krankenhaus

Güterschuppen

Steinkohlenbergbau

Dampfelektrizitätswerk

Gaswerk

Eisengießerei'

Maschinenfabrik

Metallwalzwerk

Autofedernfabrik

Gießerei NE-Metalle

Schloß- u. Schraubenfabrik

Fabrik f. Fotoapparate u. optische Instrumente

Kerzenfabrik

Galvanisierfabrik

Sägewerk

Sandgrube

Ziegelei

Mälzerei

Wasserwerk (Erdbehälter)

Kläranlage

Fabrikanlage unbekannter Art

Eisenbahnbrücke

Straßenbrücke

Fußgängerbrücke

Schleuse

Überführung eines Kanals

Planzeiger:

Zum Ablesen ist die waagerechte Teilung so an eine waagerechte Gitterlinie zu legen daß die senkrechte Teilung den zu bezeichnenden Kartenpunkt berührt Dann ist an der waagerechten Teilung bei den nächsten linken senkrechten

This is an extract from a wartime Luftwaffe map which was based on an Ordnance Survey 6in map. It was overprinted by the Germans and clearly marked with targets such as railways, bridges, steelworks and, of course, the gasworks at Pleck and the gasholder in Wolverhampton Road. (*Courtesy Mrs K. Evans*)

One of the 500lb bombs dropped by a Junkers 88 on the Pleck Gasworks on 11 November 1940 ready to be towed away for defusing. Fourth from the right is Noel Hateley GM (Works Superintendent); on his right is Fred Thickett BEM (Foreman); third from the right is Ted Bailey (Auxiliary Fire Service) and second from left, Capt Lee GC army bomb-disposal squad commander; third from left, Mr Wilson (Works Manager). Also awarded the BEM for bravery was Thomas Pearson (the first Walsall AFS member). (*M. Hateley Collection*)

R. Noel Hateley GM, Superintendent of the Corporation Gas Works, Pleck Road, 1960s. During a daylight raid on 11 November 1940, two high-explosive bombs hit the gasworks. When one pierced a gasholder, causing a fire, Noel Hateley and two men climbed up on its roof and prevented a large explosion. As a result, he was awarded the George Medal and Thomas Pearson and F. Thickett (son of Joseph Thickett, Mayor, 1923) received BEMs. (*J. Hateley*

This is a newly constructed static water tank at Crabtrees' Lincoln Works in 1942, showing the pump house with outlet pipe for topping up from the Arboretum lakes. It was situated just inside the Beacon Street/Prince's Avenue boundary. (*R. Spencer Collection*)

This shows the construction of air-raid shelters at Crabtrees in 1939 on land which had previously been tennis courts. The houses in the background were company owned at the lower end of Walhouse Road. (*R. Spencer Collection*)

Crabtrees foundry buildings showing newly applied camouflage in 1941. In addition to designing and manufacturing fuses for naval mines and certain ammunition, Crabtrees also assembled gas masks during the war. (*R. Spencer Collection*)

Officers of the 2nd Battalion South Staffordshire Regiment pictured on 15 June 1940 at Nowshera on the north-west frontier of India. Front row, left to right: Capt D. Pike, Maj Greenwood, Maj Dickens, Lt Col W.C. Green, Maj P.M. Fox, Capt F.P. Gordon, Capt C. Clark; back row: second left, 2nd Lt P.W. (Phil) Evans. (*Courtesy Mrs K. Evans*)

Lt Phil Evans in Kenya in 1943. Following a short spell with the 2nd Battalion South Staffordshire Regiment in India, he had returned to the UK for the battalion to retrain as airborne troops for D-Day, and subsequently Arnhem. Phil was sent to Kenya, however, seconded to the King's African Rifles for the rest of the war and was not involved in the airborne operations which were to result in very heavy loss of life. (*Courtesy Mrs K. Evans*)

Maj Bertie Evans OBE TD on the left, who served as Garrison Adjutant, Lichfield, from July 1940. (*Courtesy Mrs K. Evans*)

Ken Baldwin on the Arnold Pilots' Course, 1942–3. This was a scheme named after US Gen Arnold whereby RAF pilots were trained on a nine-month integrated course alongside US pilots. Here Ken is dressed in US uniform and wearing his RAF cadet's forage cap at the US Army Air Force's Advanced Flying School, Turner Field, Georgia. (*K. Baldwin Collection*)

WO Pilot Ken Baldwin. Having graduated as a pilot on 22 January 1943, Ken was posted back to the UK and trained navigators for the RAF, as well as ferrying VIPs. During the war, his wife Kath served first in the ARP and then worked three shifts a day at Featherstone filling bombs. (*K. Baldwin Collection*)

Ken Baldwin wrote home to the *Walsall Observer* while he was training in the USA, saying how fond he was of Walsall and how he was looking forward to coming home. Here he is in 2005 with both sets of his pilot's wings. The USAAF presented silver wings to pilots on passing, but Ken used the cloth RAF wings on his uniform on returning to the UK. (*K. Baldwin Collection*)

A programme for the Arnold Pilots' Reunion 2001, which included not only British but also a number of ex-pilots who travelled from the USA. (*K. Baldwin Collection*)

Flt Lt Arnold E. Pinson DFC, 1943. After the war he returned to work with Fraser Wood and Mayo, estate agents, eventually becoming senior partner and renaming the firm Fraser Wood, Mayo and Pinson. (*Courtesy Mrs S. Felgate*).

The Pinson family after Arnold's investiture with the DFC from George VI, 1943. From left to right: Jean (sister), Winifred (wife), Roger (schoolboy son), Flt Lt A.E. Pinson DFC, Phoebe (mother), Ernie (father). (*Courtesy R. Pinson*)

Flt Lt Arnold E. Pinson's DFC in 2005. This was awarded to him in 1943 for 'special duty operations' which amounted to several months flying a Wellington Mk X of 192 Squadron from Blida in North Africa at low level to reconnoitre the coasts of Sicily, Italy, Sardinia and the Toulon area, before the Allied landings. Civilian boffins were often carried as passengers to detect possible German radar installations. They wore RAF uniform in case they were shot down and fell into enemy hands – they could be shot as spies if they were in civilian clothes. (*Courtesy R. Pinson*)

F/O Malcolm Whitehouse, Eileen McBride's brother, served as navigator in 'G for George' Lancaster W4783, in 460 Squadron RAAF, seen here in 1944. He was delighted to find the plane on display many years later at Hendon RAF Museum. Navigators were originally 'observers' and some insisted on retaining the 'O' wings rather than change to an 'N'. His medal ribbon is the France and Germany Star. (*Courtesy Mr and Mrs J. McBride*)

Lancaster crew returning from a raid on Cologne on 28 June 1943 in which 608 planes flew and 25 were lost. The round trip took 4 hours 50 minutes and was the most destructive raid of the war on Cologne. The pilot was Bob Henderson, third from left, and the navigator, Malcolm Whitehouse, is just emerging. He completed twenty-nine missions by October 1943 before being posted to train others. (*Courtesy Mr and Mrs J. McBride*)

Cologne: the Hohenzollern Bridge over the Rhine, bombed, 1943. (*Courtesy Mr and Mrs J. McBride*)

Cologne bridge illustrating the accuracy of the Allied bombing, 1943. (*Courtesy Mr and Mrs J. McBride*)

Cologne cathedral, 1943. It was classed as a building of international historic importance and suffered little damage in the war. (*Courtesy Mr and Mrs J. McBride*)

Cologne, 1943. After the bridge, a major target was Cologne as a route centre which included the railway. (*Courtesy Mr and Mrs J. McBride*)

An unidentified munitions factory at Cologne that was heavily bombed, 1943. A daylight low-level raid by Blenheims in August the previous year had destroyed two power stations nearby. (*Courtesy Mr and Mrs J. McBride*)

The late Eric Fryer, an engineer with Bromford Tube, 1960s. He was ordered to report to Tilbury in 1942 where derelict wharves were being prepared for a project code-named PLUTO (pipelines under the ocean). These enabled Allied forces to be supplied with oil and petroleum after D-Day so that they could drive the Germans out of Normandy. Much of the tubing and machinery were supplied by Midland firms such as Wellman Smith Owen, Morris Cranes, ECC and Prothero Steel Tube Co. After the war, Eric became Chief Engineer and General Manager of the Talbot Tube Co. (*Courtesy Mrs M. Fryer*)

The late Mr Jack Booth, 1994. He was a sergeant in the Royal Engineers, normally glider-borne in the 6th Airborne Division. On D-Day+1 he helped relieve Pegasus Bridge and spent the next month bivouacked nearby, suffering regular German mortaring. Their task was to maintain the two bridges in good repair, filling in mortar-bomb craters and shell holes following German bombardments. Later, after the Ardennes campaign, he was mentioned in despatches for crossing open ground under fire in order to remove German explosive charges under a bridge. (*D.F. Vodden*)

This shows the original Pegasus Bridge in 1975, open for a large ship to pass along the Caen Canal. The bridge is now a museum piece, having been replaced by a similar design but with a wider roadway. (*D.F. Vodden*)

A German 20mm gun still preserved at Pegasus Bridge, 1975. This was overrun as the paratroopers cleared the Germans out of the slit trenches on the eastern bank. (*D.F. Vodden*)

The late Horace Cross on a Valentine tank at Bovington Royal Armoured Corps Depot, Dorset, where he was a training officer, *c.* 1942. (*D.F. Vodden Collection*)

This photograph was taken in July 1984 in Ellard's Drive, Wednesfield, Wolverhampton. It shows the Valentine tank which was to be restored after being bought at auction, parked opposite the factory which had been its home since 1948. Amazingly, John Pearson had started it using petrol still in it from the war in order to drive it outside to be put on a low loader. (*Courtesy J. Pearson*)

This photograph was taken in March 2004 only four weeks before the Valentine's first public appearance at Studland Bay. Although it appears to show it still being restored, the work had already been done and it was dismantled to have its old paint blasted off and new coats applied before reassembling. (*Courtesy J. Pearson*)

The Valentine DD (Duplex-Drive) tank being launched in April 2004 in Studland Bay, showing John Pearson in the turret. It was being driven by his son, Colin, and his younger son, Ian, was cranking the turret round. At that point, the waterproof screen had not been completed so it was not erected, but the water was very shallow there for the re-enactment and the DD tank did not have to float when it was launched. This event commemorated the tragedy of the losses incurred in training off Slapton Sands in 1944 before D-Day. (*Courtesy J. Pearson*)

Valentine tank restored with amphibious screen erected, 2005. The height of the screen needed periscopes to navigate by, which were designed by H.F.G. (Fred) Archenhold, a refugee from Nazi Germany. Because of its length the gun barrel had to face the rear to allow the screen to be in place for landing. (*Courtesy J. Pearson*)

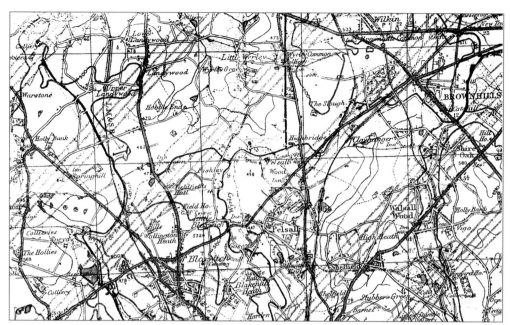

When serving with the Duke of Westminster's Dragoons on the Continent after D-Day, John Hubble was issued with maps preparatory to attacking Cleve in a Sherman flail tank in 1944. On turning over the campaign maps, he discovered they had been printed on the back of German 1:50,000 scale maps of the 1:63360 scale maps of our Ordnance Survey. This shows how the Allies had cancelled with diagonal blue lines the German version of the OS Map of Walsall. (*J. Hubble Collection*)

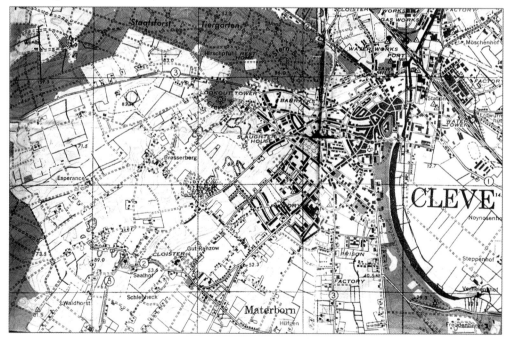

This is a section of the Allied Cleve campaign map, 1945. Corps Commander Lt Gen Brian Horrocks advanced along a narrow corridor with five divisions taking the north-west route in 21st Army Group's aim to envelope the Ruhr in conjunction with the US Army's advance from the south. (*J. Hubble Collection*)

At 11.10 a.m. on Monday, 27 November 1944, a large section of assorted explosives stored underground at RAF Fauld, near Hanbury, blew up. Excluding the nuclear explosions at Hiroshima and Nagasaki, it was the largest single detonation of the Second World War. The blast was heard as far away as Walsall, Leicester, Birmingham, Coventry and Stoke-on-Trent. A seismograph at West Bromwich, 30 miles away, registered ground tremors for several minutes, and seismographs in Geneva, Rome and Casablanca recorded the tremor. Buildings within a radius of 10 miles suffered varying amounts of damage and eighty-one lives were lost. About 3,500 to 4,000 tons of high explosive had gone up. The court of inquiry found that overfamiliarity with dangerous materials and corner-cutting procedures were to blame. The massive Tutbury crater, seen here in 1981, has been made gentler by years of weathering and tree growth. (*D.F. Vodden*)

Opposite: Sgt Wilf Sims of the Army Film and Photographic Unit, 1944. He had been in journalism since 1926 and during the war served with the Royal Signals and then with Army Public Relations, first as an observer then as picture editor with the AFPU. (*Courtesy Mrs Rita Mycock*)

Wilf Sims, pictured in Cairo in 1944, saw service from 1942 in Egypt, Iraq, Persia and Palestine. He joined Army Public Relations in Cairo in November 1943 as a sergeant observer and was appointed 'stills' editor, Army Film and Photographic Unit in Cairo in April 1944, holding that position until returning to England in April 1946 for release. He was awarded a commendation by Gen Sir Bernard Paget, C-in-C Middle East, for 'outstandingly good services' while with the Army Film and Photographic Unit. His cap badge in this picture is of the Royal Army Service Corps. (*Courtesy Mrs Rita Mycock*)

Wilf Sims in Arab costume, 1944. He wrote: 'This Arab outfit was given to one of our cameramen by King Ibn Saud of Arabia when the cameraman "covered" a visit to the King by the CIGS. Presents are always given on both sides. Facings on headdress and gallabia are pure gilt.' (*Courtesy Mrs Rita Mycock*)

Wilf Sims and colleague with hookah during a period of relaxation in Cairo, 1944. (*Courtesy Mrs Rita Mycock*)

Sgt Sims is seen here at his typewriter while serving in Cairo, 1944. (*Courtesy Mrs Rita Mycock*)

Luftwaffe map of Aldridge, 1940. It shows that the Germans had identified the airport and various limestone works as potential targets. Before the war a Royal Mail plane used to land there daily. Jack Haddock also remembers a lot of Bostons (aircraft) parked around the perimeter in the build-up to D-Day in 1943–4. (*J. Page Collection*)

Opposite top: This is a picture of Prime Minister Winston S. Churchill in the Middle East with lbn Saud taken by the Army Film and Photographic Unit, 1944. (*Courtesy Mrs Rita Mycock/Stuart Williams*)

Opposite bottom: Clearly Sgt Wilf Sims and fellow members of the Army Film and Photographic Unit had some time for relaxation, so they took this picture of the Sphinx, 1945. (*Courtesy Mrs Rita Mycock/Stuart Williams*)

Linley Cavern, Aldridge, was formerly a wartime bomb store and is pictured here in 1955. It is now buried under S. Jones's Transport Depot. (*R.A. Brevitt*)

Phil Wood – Bevin boy at the Miners' Hostel, Sheffield, 1945. Ernest Bevin had master-minded the scheme for one in ten of conscripts to be sent down the mines, where they served in support or transport services to the coal face. Because mining had not been a reserved occupation, miners had been called up to serve in the Armed Forces, which led to an acute shortage of coal at a time when the country was almost completely dependent on it for heating, lighting and energy. (*Courtesy C.P.J. Wood*)

Bevin Boys' reunion at Littleton Colliery, Cannock, on Armistice Day 1993. They were part of the 10 per cent of national call-up boys who were sent down the mines whether they liked it or not. Extreme left is former Walsall Mayor, Phil Wood. (*Courtesy C.P.J. Wood*)

Bevin Boys march down the Mall on 19 August 1995 to celebrate VJ day. Phil Wood carries the banner. (*Courtesy C.P.J. Wood*)

Prince Bernhard takes the salute on 2 June 1945 at Oldebroek Barracks near Kampen, on the shores of the Zuyder Zee. (*J. Hubble Collection*)

Prince Bernhard shakes hands with John Hubble, 2 June 1945. (*J. Hubble Collection*)

Capt John Hubble, Air Liaison Officer with 140 Wing, RAF Gütersloh, 1946. From left to right: pilot Eric Caesar-Gordon, John Hubble and navigator Desmond ? by the Möhne See. (*J. Hubble Collection*)

A view of a Mosquito taken from another Mosquito by John Hubble just after the war, in 1946. (*J. Hubble*)

Trainee radar mechanics at HMS *Royal Arthur*, which was in the former, quite new, Butlins holiday camp at Skegness, July 1944. (*H.R. Taylor Collection*)

HMS *Colossus*, a 17,000-ton light aircraft carrier, was launched in December 1944, destined for the Far East for operations against the Japanese, but didn't reach Sydney until VJ day. She was later loaned, then sold to France and renamed *Arromanches*. Roy Taylor served on her from December 1945 to June 1946. (*H.R. Taylor Collection*)

HMS *Jamaica* was an 8,000-ton cruiser,
shown here leaving Trincomalee harbour in
1946. (*H.R. Taylor Collection*)

H.R. Taylor, a radar specialist, standing by a 6in
gun on board HMS *Jamaica* in September 1946,
having joined her in August. (*H.R. Taylor
Collection*)

3

The Anglo-American Week

Anglo-American Friendship Week, February 1945. The Mayor, Cllr John Whiston, held office from 1944 to 1945 and was created a Freeman of the Borough on 1 May 1956. (*G. Whiston Collection*)

Mrs W. Whiston, daughter-in-law of the Mayor, with US politicians apparently outside the town hall in February 1945 during the Anglo-American Friendship Week. (*G. Whiston Collection*)

This Anglo-American Friendship Week notice was displayed on The Bridge in February, 1945. (*G. Whiston Collection*)

American troops visit Mark Cross, February 1945. This venue was probably chosen because the firm was founded in Boston, Massachusetts, in 1845 by Mark's father, an Irish saddler called Henry Cross. (*G. Whiston Collection*)

Leather workers at Mark Cross, February 1945. The firm's association with Walsall arose from its importing Walsall-made saddlery and leather goods. The firm's owner in 1908 was Patrick Murphy, who had been an apprentice in Walsall. He bought out his Walsall supplier that year, together with its factory in Warewell Street. (*G. Whiston Collection*)

Mrs 'Tiny' Hounslow making wallets at Mark Cross Leathergoods, watched by GIs, February 1945. (*G. Whiston Collection*)

The Mark Cross advertisement of 1949 shows its establishment as 1845, and its US address as 707 Fifth Avenue. They were clearly very much into manufacturing high-quality, fancy leather goods such as wallets and jewellery cases. (*John Griffiths Collection*)

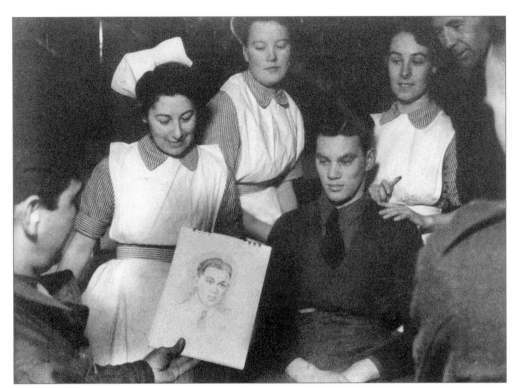

A GI draws a portrait of a British serviceman in Manor Hospital, February 1945. (*G. Whiston Collection*)

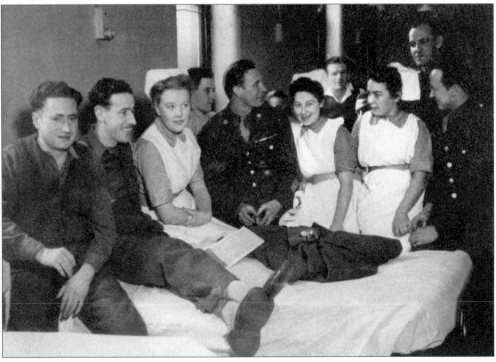

British wounded servicemen in Manor Hospital, February 1945. Quite a few were repatriated former prisoners of war. (*G. Whiston Collection*)

GIs visit Frank Ringrose Saddlery works in Midland Road, February 1945. (*G. Whiston Collection*)

GIs are served with light refreshments in the lobby of the George Hotel, February 1945. (*G. Whiston Collection*)

As part of the Anglo-American Friendship Week celebrations there was a wardens' party in Pattisons' Tea Room, where the Mayor made a short speech, February 1945. (*G. Whiston Collection*)

ANGLO-AMERICAN FRIENDSHIP WEEK.

AN INVITATION DANCE
(under the patronage of his Worship the Mayor)

WILL BE HELD AT

THE GEORGE HOTEL, WALSALL,

on FRIDAY, FEBRUARY 23rd, 1945.

Dancing 9 p.m. to Midnight.

THE DANCE BAND OF THE 10TH REPLACEMENT DEPÔT
(by kind permission of Commanding Officer).

Organiser :
MRS. B. HODSON.   TICKETS 10/- each.   EVENING DRESS.

A copy of the official invitation to a celebratory dance at the George Hotel, February 1945. (*G. Whiston Collection*)

Lt Col Sleeper arrives at the George Hotel for the dinner dance, February 1945. (*G. Whiston Collection*)

Lt Col Sleeper with Mr and Mrs Hobson, who organised the dinner dance in the George Hotel, February 1945. (*G. Whiston Collection*)

Mayor, Cllr John Whiston, making his speech in the Arboretum, February 1945. He stressed the quality of the friendship between the Americans and the people of Walsall. (*G. Whiston Collection*)

To mark the occasion, the Mayor presented new colours to the Americans, February 1945. (*G. Whiston Collection*)

After their presentation, the US colours were proudly displayed in the Commanding Officer's office. (*G. Whiston Collection*)

Col Kilian's hand-painted Christmas card for 1944 which was sent to the Mayor, Cllr John Whiston. (*G. Whiston Collection*)

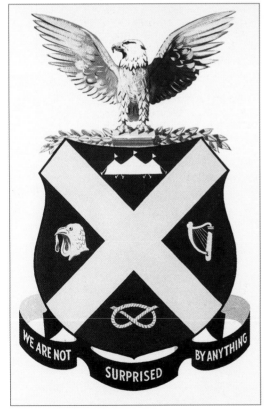

Col James Kilian, commander of the US Army 10th Replacement Depot, who liaised with the Mayor to establish good relationships between his men and the townspeople, February 1945. Because he was recalled urgently to the USA to face charges concerning his conduct as commander, a suitably inscribed silver tureen could not be presented to him at a celebratory luncheon in the town hall. The silver remains in the Mayor's Parlour, while Col Kilian, apparently cleared of the charges, is buried at Arlington Military Cemetery. Details of the case are in Jack Gieck, *Lichfield–The US Army on Trial*, Akron, Ohio, University of Akron Press, 1997. (*G. Whiston Collection*)

10th US Army Replacement Depot badge with the motto 'We are not surprised by anything', which seems ironic in the light of the court martial of Col Kilian and others for ill-treatment of prisoners in the military prison. (*G. Whiston Collection*)

HEADQUARTERS
CONTINENTAL BASE SECTION
U. S. FORCES EUROPEAN THEATER

APO 807
24 September 1946

Major B. Evans, British Army
c/o Midland Bank
Walsall / England

Dear Major Evans:

 Now that the Bad Nauheim chapter of the Lichfield
trials is closing, I want to take this opportunity to
acknowledge and thank you for your help and support.
Your appearance as a witness (or your deposition) was of
great assistance in securing a partial vindication, not
only for myself and others involved, but also in clearing
the name of the old 10th Depot, an organization which we
all know did a superior job and contributed greatly to
the success of our Armed Forces.

 The verdict of the court in my case was disappoint-
ing to me because in the first place the incidents alleg-
ed against the 10th Depot are not true. I hope in the
future we will be able to prove this to the public and to
show everyone that the 10th Depot was not a small stockade
of horrors enclosed in barbed wire, but was a large Replacement Depot composed of personnel imbued with the spirit
to do their duty under any and all circumstances.

 Again thanking you for your contribution and
assistance and knowing that I can continue to rely upon
your assistance in any future efforts that might neces-
sarily be made to clear the name of the 10th Depot, I am

Very sincerely yours,

This letter from Col Kilian was written in September 1946 after his court martial and thanks
Maj Bertie Evans for his support. Maj Evans was Garrison Adjutant at Whittington and also
liaison officer between the British Army and British civilians such as the Mayor and people of
Walsall. (*Courtesy Mrs K. Evans*)

A group of US soldiers of the 10th Replacement Unit who were billeted on the recently built Pheasey Estate, 1943. The new houses had first been used by British soldiers returning from Dunkirk, followed by members of the Pioneer Corps, before this US unit was photographed in 1943 facing the community centre which they used as their HQ. The small schoolboy in the background is Bill Newman who grew up to become a JP and Mayor of Walsall. (*E.W. Newman Collection*)

Men of the 10th Replacement Unit of the US Army marched past the saluting dais in front of the Council House where the Commanding Officer, Lt Col Sleeper, and the Mayor, Cllr John Whiston, took the salute, February 1945. (*G. Whiston Collection*)

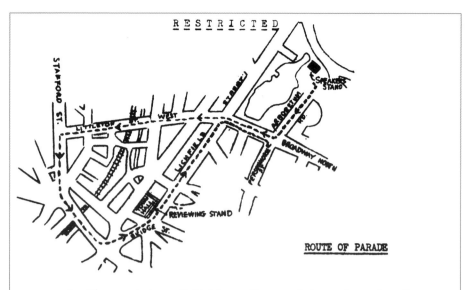

<u>R E S T R I C T E D</u>

ROUTE OF PARADE

    d.   16 paces between Battalions, 12 paces between Companies, 8 paces
between Platoons.
    e.   Each Battalion will consist of two Companies of two Platoons each.
    f.   A Platoon will consist of 50 men, 4 men abreast, 12 men deep, and
front and rear guide.
    g.   Positions will be taken on the Green in order from right to left,
facing the speaker's stand, - Band and Drum and Bugle Corps, 4th Bn., 49th Bn.,
37th Bn., 44th Bn., and 98th Bn.

The map of the march past for February 1945 was classified 'Restricted', although the
end of the war was less than three months away. (*G. Whiston Collection*)

The Mayor, Cllr John Whiston, taking the salute, February 1945. (*G. Whiston Collection*)

The Mayor, Cllr John Whiston, is seen here with Vera Lynn, who came to Walsall to sing during the Anglo-American Friendship Week, February 1945. (*G. Whiston Collection*).

The Mayor making his speech at the dinner for US and Walsall lawyers, 7 March 1945. (*G. Whiston Collection*)

This shows Walsall solicitors and US lawyers at a joint dinner from which sprang the Walsall Law Association, 7 March 1945. The association has just celebrated its diamond jubilee. From left to right: J.L. Dilcock, US lawyer, Maj H.B. Evans OBE TD, South Staffordshire Regiment and Garrison Adjutant, J.H. Sherborne. W. Staley Brooks is in the background while in the foreground are A.V. Haden and E.W. Haden. (*G. Whiston Collection*)

Judge Tucker speaks at the dinner during which he gave a lucid explanation of the working of the House of Lords in the English judicial system, 7 March 1945. (*G. Whiston Collection*)

This 1931 Bentley underwent conversion into a snack-bar to provide food after air raids in such city centres as Coventry. The photograph was taken in 1939 and shows Sir Cliff Tibbits as Mayor and Cllr John Whiston (second from right), the future Mayor in 1944–5. Both were subsequently made Freemen of the Borough on May Day, 1956. (*G. Whiston Collection*)

A wartime bus shelter on The Bridge in 1945. Queueing passengers were protected from falling shrapnel by the corrugated-iron roofing. (*G. Whiston Collection*)

4

Victory & Beyond

This picture of St Matthew's Church shows it floodlit to celebrate the end of the war in Europe in May 1945. (*D.F. Vodden Collection*)

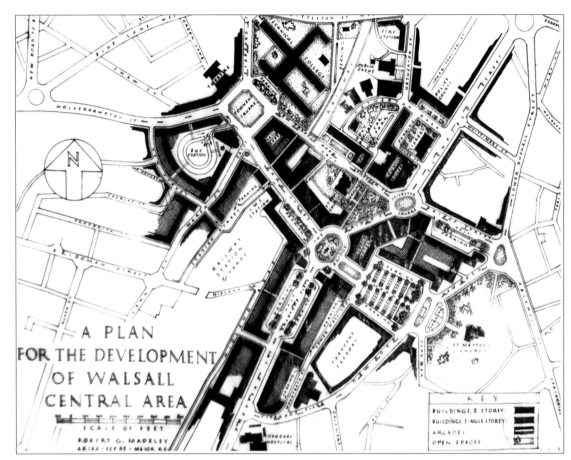

The Town Council published ideas for a new town plan in 1945. Local architect and designer of the Savoy Cinema, Maj R.G. (Rob) Madeley, serving in the Royal Engineers in the Far East, offered this comment: 'It is difficult to see, except for the traffic roads, any clear-cut guiding principles, any community centres or obviously planned grouping . . . future developments appear to be little more than extensions of the existing straggles.' (*Courtesy C. Madeley*)

Built before the war in 1937 to the designs of R.G. Madeley FRIBA, the Savoy Cinema is seen here at the top of Park Street in 1946. (*D.F. Vodden Collection*)

The Grand Theatre was destroyed by fire in
June 1939. The Theatre Bar was established
on the same site and is seen here in 1946.
(*D.F. Vodden Collection*)

Another picture of the Grand Theatre at
the corner of Station Street and Park
Street before the disastrous fire in 1939.
(*D.F. Vodden Collection*)

A view of Temple Street in 1946. In earlier times it
was known as 'Crooked Alley', as the houses as
well as the road were crooked. It was eventually
renamed but disappeared soon after this
photograph was taken when Church Hill was
cleared for redevelopment. (*D.F. Vodden Collection*)

Soon after the war, in 1947, the ground around
Upper Rushall Street was cleared in order to
landscape the area around St Matthew's Church.
(*R.A. Brevitt*)

While taking these pictures of ground clearance in Upper Rushall Street in 1947, the photographer received strong objections from the workforce! (*R.A. Brevitt*)

Blue Coat School prefects, 1946–7. Back row, left to right: Stephen Hobson, Elsie Burton, Betty Swift, Jean Lovett, Brenda Brooks, Lawrence Hogg. Middle row: John Newton, Leslie Williams, Douglas Lovett, William Astbury, Terry Harrison. Front row: -?- Hilda Brooks, Anne Clarke, -?-, -?-, -?-. (*Courtesy T. Harrison*)

Bluecoat Old Blues Association on a ramble, 1952. The teachers include Freda Blanchard and Horace James. (*Courtesy T. Harrison*)

St Matthew's spire restoration, 1949. This was a major restoration and the spire was rebuilt in red sandstone from about 6ft up from the parapet of the tower. The work was completed in time for Coronation year, 1953. (*D.F. Vodden Collection*)

Workmen fixing the 12ft-high cross on St Matthew's new spire at the end of its restoration in 1953. This involved two attempts because the first thread was wrong! (*R.A. Brevitt*)

St Matthew's Church from the north showing how the hill had been cleared of housing and the surrounding area landscaped by the 1960s. (*B. Felgate Collection*)

Hatherton Road Congregational Church with spire, 1949. This was regarded as dangerous after some stone flaked off and fell on the pavement, so the spire was dismantled in 1949. (*R.A. Brevitt*)

Hatherton Road Congregational Church, now the United Reformed Church, minus spire, 2005. Notable members who attended in the past included Joseph Leckie, a former Mayor, alderman and MP. (*D.F. Vodden*)

Freer Street, with Brace Windle Blyth & Co., fancy leather goods manufacturers in Goodall Street, the site now occupied by the telephone exchange, 1952. The Stores public house was later the Pen and Wig and is currently Tommy's Bar. The *Walsall Observer* vehicle is parked outside the *Observer* Printing Works with Jim Wood, the driver. (*R.A. Brevitt*)

Eylands works in Lower Rushall Street used to manufacture buckles, including the Boy Scout belt buckle and the famous 'S' belt buckle, as well as swivel hooks and 'D' rings, both for waist belts and harnesses. It is seen here in 1952 before restoration. (*J. Griffiths Collection*)

Not long after the end of the war there was a hard winter, as these deep snowdrifts in Stafford Road, Bloxwich, in 1947 show. (*G.J. Clark*)

The winter of 1962/3 was very severe and the lakes in the Arboretum froze over. It was planned to have an ice-skating gala there in the spring but a thaw set in before it could be held. These ice hockey goals are on the main Hatherton Lake in January 1963. (*R.A. Brevitt*)

As the ice was so thick, many Walsall people took advantage of it including the skaters seen on the lake in January 1963. (*R.A. Brevitt*)

This view of High Street in the snow in 1951 reminds us of severe winters in the past, and also that vehicles could be parked on non-market days among the stalls. (*R.A. Brevitt*)

Hill Street and Hawleys' leather goods factory in the shadow of St Matthew's Church, 1946. During the war they had made bomber jackets and flying helmets. (*R.A. Brevitt*)

Hill Street before 1963. Not a great deal of change between these two views although, more recently, a group of apartments has been built in the shadow of the church. (*R.A. Brevitt*)

This gas lamp, seen here in 1951, stood in Bath Street; it was unusual in that it incorporated a fire hydrant. (*R.A. Brevitt*)

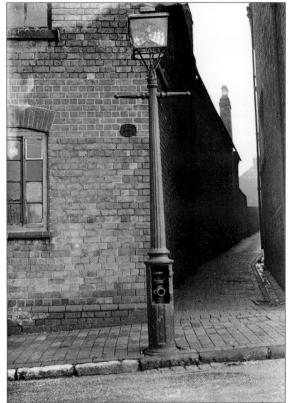

Pole squatter Vic Reeves outside the New Yorker, Broadway North, 1952. The owner, Charles Teakle, was hosting this attempt to break a world record to promote his restaurant. Later, in 1957, he was prosecuted for holding dances on Sundays without a club licence. (*R.A. Brevitt*)

FESTIVAL   OF   BRITAIN   1951

PAGEANT
OF
WALSALL

Written and Devised
by
CHARLES   BARDELL

TOWN HALL, WALSALL.   8th to 13th October, 1951

Festival of Britain Pageant of Walsall, October 1951. It presented the story of Walsall and was written by Charles Bardell. It covered the earliest mention of Walsall in 916, through the Middle Ages, the Tudor and Stuart periods, Wesley's visit in 1743, to the deputation to the Prince of Wales in 1794 protesting that his fashion for shoe laces was destroying buckle-making. The story of the nursing career of Sister Dora was covered by a tableau of three episodes. (*J. Griffiths Collection*)

Some Festival of Britain Pageant of Walsall players in Leicester Street by the town hall in 1951. (*R.A. Brevitt*)

The Arboretum illuminations were revived as part of Walsall's Festival of Britain celebrations in 1951, with tasteful lighting of trees and shrubs designed by Jim Winton, Head of Parks and Gardens. Subsequently, second-hand lights were obtained from Blackpool but now Walsall designs and displays its own lights as a major tourist attraction. (*R.A. Brevitt*)

These floral arrangements in the entrance to the Council House and the town hall were designed by Jim Winton and constructed by his Parks and Gardens staff for the Queen's visit in 1962. A letter of appreciation was subsequently sent from Buckingham Palace. (*Mrs P. Winton Collection*)

On 1 May 1951, the Mayor, W.R. Wheway, escorted Princess Margaret when she visited his chain-making works. She said afterwards that she was interested in machinery of all kinds and was very pleased to be given a crocodile handbag before she left the town. During the war, Wheways had been a manufacturer of chains for flail tanks used for clearing minefields. (*R.A. Brevitt*)

Also on 1 May 1951, Princess Margaret unveiled the plaque in the Memorial Gardens on Church Hill in the presence of the Mayor, W.R. Wheway. (*Courtesy Mrs P. Winton*)

A Walsall workshop which was no better than a 'lean-to' shed, 1956. Three girls would have worked here. Notice the teapot on the table for them to make their own tea. The bowl was for hand-washing; there was no running hot water so it would have been boiled in the kettle. Also in the picture are three welding machines. (*D.F. Vodden Collection*)

D. Mason & Sons' exhibition stand at the British Industries Fair, Castle Bromwich, 1950s. From 1902, the firm operated in Wisemore, in a building that now houses the Leather Museum. In 1919, they moved to Marsh Street where their premises and those occupied by Whitehouse Cox have since been converted to apartments. (*R.A. Brevitt*)

Handford Greatrex stand at the British Industries Fair, Castle Bromwich, in the 1950s. Handford Greatrex & Co. of Springhill Road was one of the oldest tanneries in Walsall. A major supplier to Clark's Shoes, they were taken over by Harvey's of Nantwich and closed down three years later in 1964. (*R.A. Brevitt*)

This was the main reception area and stairs at Crabtrees' Lincoln Works in Beacon Street in 1926. The newell posts had been carved personally by the founder and are currently in a museum store, having been rescued before the building's demolition. (*D.F. Vodden*)

J.A. Crabtree's medallion, dating from 1926, bears his motto: 'That which is built soundly endures well'. He had established his electrical switches firm in Upper Rushall Street in 1919 and moved to Beacon Street in 1926. A brilliant man and a good employer, he died prematurely in 1935 aged 49. (*Crabtrees Society Collection*)

This is the medallion of John Crabtree, son of the founder, and dates from 1958. Too young to work when his father died, he came into the firm after graduating from Queen's College, Oxford, and joined the Board in 1944. He later became Chairman and Managing Director in 1958. His motto was 'By Wisdom and Prudence'. (*Crabtrees Society Collection*)

Crabtrees Sales Conference, 1969. Crabtrees were involved in worldwide trade at their peak and this conference brought together the key members of the sales team. (*T. Harrison Collection*)

Walsall Locks and Cart Gear Ltd, 1950. The firm was situated in Neale Street, off Hollyhedge Lane, Walsall, which was named after Edward Vansittart Neale, a prominent member of the Co-operative Movement, who opened the works in 1892. They manufactured padlocks, rim locks and latches, cabinet locks, car door locks, cylinder locks and latches, and safe locks as well as hames, chains and spring hooks for harnesses. They were known locally as the 'Co-op Locks' and had a social club and an on-site sports facility. (*H.R. Taylor Collection*)

This aerial view of the power station was taken using a cumbersome plate camera in 1952. Although building started before the war, it was considerably extended soon afterwards. (*R.A. Brevitt*)

The former power station at Reedswood, 1952. It used to dominate Walsall's western horizon. It has now been developed as a retail park and domestic housing. (*R.A. Brevitt*)

This is a view of the former power station at Reedswood, taken from beside the canal in about 1960. The canal was used to supply the power station with coal. (*B. Felgate Collection*)

Walsall power station, 1952. (*Rex Stone*)

This shows an aspect of the Old Square redevelopment in 1967. It looks across from the bottom of High Street towards Freer Street where the former Pen and Wig – now Tommy's Bar – is visible. (*Courtesy D. Wilkins, First House Photography*)

This 1967 view of the Old Square redevelopment looks down the slope towards the former cinema and the Dirty Duck public house in Leicester Square. The bell tower in Tower Street is also visible. (*Courtesy D. Wilkins, First House Photography*)

Looking down the market and High Street,
c. 1960 should be compared with the view
below, taken about twenty years later.
(*B. Felgate Collection*)

This view from St Matthew's Church steps
down the market was taken in about 1980 by
Terry Harrison. Unlike the previous picture it
shows the power station cooling towers to the
right. At the top of Park Street is the Townend
Crown building, with the Overstrand halfway
down High Street. (*T. Harrison*)

The site in Tower Street being cleared for the new Gala Baths, 1953. This is currently being largely pedestrianised for the creation of the new Civic Quarter. (*Courtesy Mrs N. Hilton*)

This photograph, taken from the Council House bell tower in 1953, shows the fire station in Darwall Street and the site for the Gala Baths. The Gala Baths were built in 1960 and the Civic Centre was opened in 1976. (*R.A. Brevitt*)

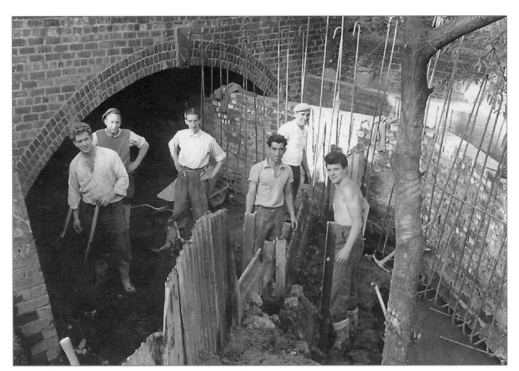

Workmen preparing the site for the Gala Baths, 1959. The workers have exposed the 'Walsall Water' which runs under the town from the north and emerges the other side of Leicester Street, before going underground again under the new Civic Square. (*Courtesy Mrs N. Hilton*)

The mayoral party led by the Mayor, Cllr A.V. Fletcher, entering the Gala Baths building at the official opening in 1960. (*Courtesy Mrs N. Hilton*)

This photograph of The Bridge was taken before 1957 and shows the original white marble statue of Sister Dora which was replaced in bronze in 1957 (see below). The railings used to surround the entrance to the public conveniences, formerly underground. (*D.F. Vodden Collection*)

The modern bronze statue of Sister Dora outside the George Hotel, which occupied the site of her first hospital, 1957. The George was demolished in 1979 to make way for Tesco and the Halifax. In the conversion of The Bridge to the Civic Square, Sister Dora's statue was moved to the opposite side next to Lloyds TSB. (*R.A. Brevitt*)

Unveiling the bronze statue of Sister Dora took place on her birthday, 16 January, in 1957. The original statue was carved by Francis Williamson in white Sicilian marble and unveiled on 11 October 1886, but was later damaged by atmospheric corrosion. (*R.A. Brevitt*)

Unveiling Sister Dora by Vice-chairman, J.N.F. Cotterell, of the Walsall Hospital Management Committee, who had witnessed the original being unveiled in 1886, with Walsall Mayor, Danny Cartwright, and visiting mayors of Richmond and Redcar from Sister Dora's home county of Yorkshire. The Matron may be Miss A.M. Swain. (*R.A. Brevitt*)

These are pillars from the former George Hotel. When the George was dismantled in May 1979 after eight years standing empty, these columns were dumped for a time at the Parks and Gardens Department at Gorway. They originally graced the outside of the former Fisherwick Hall near Whittington. (*R.A. Brevitt*)

The General Hospital front entrance, 1978. This hospital was built as the result of Sister Dora's initiative but she was too ill to attend the original opening in 1878 and died on Christmas Eve that year. (*Courtesy T. Highfield*)

The General Hospital rear entrance approached from Glebe Street, 1978. (*Courtesy T. Highfield*)

Goscote Hospital, seen here from the air, was established originally as an isolation hospital in 1930. It has been used in more recent times as a geriatric hospital and as a rehabilitation unit; it is now earmarked for the proposed Walsall Hospice. (*Courtesy T. Highfield*)

This was the station entrance from Park Street in 1972. Built just after the First World War by LMS as a prestige building, it was a much-loved landmark building in the centre of town. (*Photo D. Burwell*)

Station Street entrance, 1972. (*Photo D. Burwell*)

Station and yards, 1972. (*Photo D. Burwell*)

The railway yards in Midland Road were laid out on the site of the former racecourse. They in turn have now been replaced by a retail park currently earmarked to serve the Bradford Place bus traffic. (*Photo D. Burwell*)

The station entrance, just before demolition, 1978. (*D.F. Vodden*)

Traffic in Lower Bridge Street was photographed in 1960 from the *Observer* office window. This is one-way now and is restricted to public transport. (*R.A. Brevitt*)

The *Walsall Observer* offices in Lower Bridge Street, decorated for the Coronation of Queen Elizabeth II in 1953. (*R.A. Brevitt*)

Following his demobilisation from the army, Wilf Sims returned to work at the *Walsall Observer* and is seen here in his office in 1951. (*Courtesy the* Walsall Observer/*Craig Winyard/Stuart Williams*)

Hydesville Tower School, 1955. (*Hydesville School Collection*)

Hydesville Tower School Staff, 1971. Front row, left to right: Mrs J. Anderson, Mrs E. Taylor, Miss D. Bryan, Mr W. Flood, Mrs B. Cheetham, Mr R. Hopkins, Mrs G. Spencer. Middle row: Mrs G. Carver, Mrs M. Dewley, Mrs M. Neale, Mrs M. Jones, Mrs N. Needham, Mrs B. Wootton, Mrs J. Garner, Mr A. Beetlestone. Back row: Miss J. Mildren, Mrs G. Clamp, Mrs P. Burton, -?-, Mrs Z. Jackson, Mrs D. Cope, Mrs J. Hough. (*Hydesville Tower School Collection*)

5

Scouting for Boys

This shows part of Walsall Sea Scouts' water display on the Arboretum lake during Walsall Scout Week, May 1946. (*Walsall Sea Scouts/B. Griffiths*)

Bottom boards for the new guard ship *Pole Star* are shown here laid at Worseys boatyard, Bloxwich Road, with the troop's good friend, Mr Worsey, on 31 May 1944. (*Walsall Sea Scouts/B. Griffiths*)

Skipper Halliwell fixing the words 'Walsall Sea Scouts' on 23 July 1944. (*Walsall Sea Scouts/B. Griffiths Collection*)

Sea Scouts' guard ship *Pole Star*, 1945. This ship is permanently moored and acts as HQ for the Sea Scouts. (*Walsall Sea Scouts/B. Griffiths*)

Soon after launching, *Pole Star* became locked in by the frozen surface of Powell's Pool, 1947. (*Walsall Sea Scouts/B. Griffiths*)

This shows the new guard ship *Pole Star* on a low loader on its way to Powell's Pool, Sutton Park, on 5 August 1944. (*Walsall Sea Scouts/B. Griffiths*)

Lord Rowallan, Chief Scout, launches the 3rd Walsall Sea Scouts guard ship *Pole Star*, 1954. (*Walsall Sea Scouts/B. Griffiths*)

The *Pole Star*'s first crew, 1948. Back row, left to right: J. Gadsby, R. Pace, G. Langley, N. Lord. Third row: R. Johns, R. Stebbins, G. Turner, F. Homer. Second row: Jos Carver (Instructor), J. Halliwell (Scoutmaster), L. Stanley (Group Scoutmaster), R. Kenyon (Instructor). Front row: P. Halliwell, P. Dobson, G. Millard, G. Grimley, P. Hall. (*Walsall Sea Scouts/B. Griffiths*)

3rd Walsall Sea Scouts resting on the way home from Nottingham to Walsall in 1953. The outward journey had been 80 miles by kayak from Rugeley as part of the National Scout Canoe Cruise. (*Walsall Sea Scouts/B. Griffiths*)

Scoutmaster Leonard G. Stanley (Sarge) at Bala
Camp in 1954 who was the driving force as
Scoutmaster of the 3rd Walsall Sea Scouts. He ran
the family buckle-making business first in Brace
Street and later in Brockhurst Crescent; he was
also a talented artist and amateur film-maker.
(*Walsall Sea Scouts/ B. Griffiths*)

August Camp, Bala, 1949. Back row, left to right:
Horice, Recco, Tony, Trevor, Tom and Roy Pace, Big
Massa, Steph, B. Griffiths, P. Halliwell. Middle row:
Mic, Ging, Sarge, Jos, Bottle. Front row:
G. Matthews, Bill, Peach, P. Marriott, K. Shenton,
R. Plummer, H. Penwell, Spider Webb. The latter,
Robin Webb, having competed in a regatta on Lake
Ontario in 1970, was selected twenty-four years
after this picture was taken to represent Great
Britain in a four-man crew at Seattle, then in the
individual championships at San Francisco and
finally, in the North American Championships
regatta. (*Walsall Sea Scouts/ B. Griffiths*)

Summer camp, 1953. Back row, left to right: Mills, Goode, Kirby, Allport, Pace. Middle row: Gibbs, McKie, Sarge, Longmore. Front row: Grant, Briars, Nicholas, Brown. David Brown always preferred batting in the nets to sea scouting – on 4 September 1982 he was interviewed on radio as manager of the Warwickshire Cricket Team. (*Walsall Sea Scouts/B. Griffiths*)

This poster colour painting of a typical Sea Scout was done by Sarge (Leonard Stanley) and is the frontispiece for the 1944 logbook. (*Walsall Sea Scouts/B. Griffiths*)

Second cruise in *Morna*, 1954. Nine members of the 3rd Walsall Sea Scouts enjoyed a fourteen-day cruise in the Channel aboard the 22-ton ketch *Morna* covering 560 miles, the most ambitious yet undertaken by the troop. They were led by scoutmasters Jos Carver and Peter Hall. The route included Yarmouth I-o-W, Weymouth, Torquay, Cherbourg, Guernsey, Jersey and St Malo. (*Walsall Sea Scouts/B. Griffiths*)

St George's Day Scout Movement parade in High Street, *c.* 1950. In the centre is Alf Felgate, Scout Commissioner. Along the sides of High Street are many now long-lost shops and buildings. (*B. Felgate Collection*)

The Leckie Shield was awarded to the troop who performed best in competition every year. The Scouts chose the nature of the competition which could cover camping, hiking, sports and other suitable activities. This is the winning team in 1950. (*B. Felgate Collection*)

Sea Scouts with shield and pennants, 1971. Back row, left to right: Ian Cooke, Clive Done, Richard Hinton, Alan Jones, John Plater, -?- Jones. Middle row: Neal Plater, Richard Griffiths, David Harrington. Front row: Geoff Brians, Ralf Nickless. (*Walsall Sea Scouts/B. Griffiths*)

Members of the 16th Walsall (St Matthew's Own) Scout team with the Leckie Shield, which they won at Beaudesert camp in competition with other Walsall Scout troops in 1951. The teams were judged in camping and general scouting activities by Mr J.K. Davies, Assistant County Commissioner. (*B. Felgate Collection*)

Winners of the Leckie Shield group at St Matthew's, 1951. (*B. Felgate Collection*)

In 1963 the 16th Walsall (St Matthew's Own) Scout Group celebrated their fortieth anniversary. The Bishop of Stafford, the Rt Revd R.G. Clitherow, dedicated new colours. Alderman Sir Cliff Tibbits, President of the District Scouts Association, is in the centre; he had been Mayor in 1939 and 1940. (*B. Felgate Collection*)

A.J. Felgate, Scout Commissioner, with the Revd Vernon Nicholls, Vicar of St Matthew's and future Bishop of Sodor and Man. (*B. Felgate Collection*)

Brian Felgate receives his Queen's Scout badge from the Commissioner in 1955. (*B. Felgate Collection*)

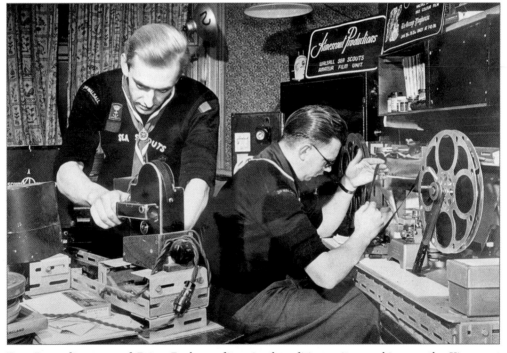

Tom Pace, director, and Brian Beebee, editor, in the editing suite, working on the Kinescout film *V.I.P.* in November 1952. This was submitted for the 'Ten Best Films of 1952' competition arranged by *The Amateur Cineworld* and was shown at the Grange Theatre in January 1953. (*Walsall Sea Scouts/B. Griffiths*)

Lord Rowallan, the Chief Scout, at the *Walsall Observer* offices at the time of the World Scout Jamboree, August 1957. (*R.A. Brevitt*)

HM The Queen at the World Scout Jamboree at Sutton Park in August 1957. (*R.A. Brevitt*)

HRH Prince Philip at the World Scout Jamboree in August 1957, talking to Scout leaders. (*R.A. Brevitt*)

The Chief Scout, Lord Rowallan, is greeted at the World Scout Jamboree following heavy rain, judging by his wellington boots, August 1957. (*P.J. Hall*)

St George's Day, 1958. 29th Walsall Cubs parading to St Matthew's Church, led by Cubmaster Terry Harrison. (*T. Harrison Collection*)

Scout Commissioner A.J. Felgate's Silver Acorn was awarded on St George's Day, 1968, for his considerable service to the Scout Movement over many years. (*B. Felgate Collection*)

The 3rd Walsall Sea Scouts' logbook is bound in leather, as is appropriate for a Walsall troop. The 1948 cover has the Olympic Games symbol on it because a detachment of the troop went to Torquay to help steward the sailing Olympics, which were held in Torbay that summer. (*Walsall Sea Scouts/B. Griffiths*)

6

Leisure & Recreation

Opening the Lido in the Arboretum in August 1953. The Lido was provided through the generosity of the Chairman of the Walsall Show and Fête Committee, Alderman John Whiston OBE. The memorial clock was donated in 1963 by the South Staffordshire Branch of the Electrical Contractors' Association, through his Worship the Mayor, H.F. Truman JP. Mr Truman's electrical shop was in Bridge Street near the Chocolate Box. (*R.A. Brevitt*)

The first bathers in the Lido at the Arboretum. (*R.A. Brevitt*)

The Borough Police gave regular Christmas parties for local children in the 1950s and 1960s. On this particular occasion they were entertained by a chimps' tea party. (*R.J. Meller Collection*)

Walsall Rotary Club members picnicking in Sutton Park with Rotarian John Wiggin in the foreground, 1960s. (*H.R. Taylor*)

Queen Mary's Schools in Lichfield Street, pre-1965. Built in 1850 as the Grammar School for Boys, the buildings also housed the Girls' High School from its foundation in 1893. The need for a new school in Sutton Road was recognised in the 1930s but the war intervened. Although pre-war plans had been made for new buildings for the High School, these were reversed and the boys moved into the new school in 1965. (*C. Hollingsworth Collection*)

Bertie Evans at Mayfield, summer 1952.
On his retirement he went to live in
Cornwall for a short time but didn't settle
and returned to Walsall. He died on
22 June 1956 after a long illness, aged 65.
(*Courtesy Mrs K. Evans*)

Queen Mary's Grammar School, Sutton
Road, from the air, under construction,
March 1964. (*Courtesy QMGS Archive*)

Dr Cornwell, the first Principal of the new West Midlands Training College, welcoming some of the first students in 1963. These buildings, residences and the Teaching Tower are currently planned for demolition and replacement by the present owners, Wolverhampton University. (*D.F. Vodden Collection*)

The Lord Lieutenant of the West Midlands, Lord Aylesford, arrives at West Midlands College of Higher Education to preside over the graduation ceremony in 1979, and is being greeted by the Principal's wife, Mrs Joan Cornwell. (*D.F. Vodden Collection*)

The Who at a regular Walsall town hall concert. At the time they included John Entwistle, Keith Moon and Roger Daltrey. (*David Wilkins*)

The Beatles and Walsall girl fans who had won a competition to meet them on the *Lucky Star Show* at the ATV Studios, Birmingham, mid-1960s. (*David Wilkins*)

Stevie Winwood, who was born in Handsworth, played in the Spencer Davis Group and The Traffic and is seen here at a Walsall town hall concert. (*David Wilkins*)

Members of the Staffordshire Regimental Association in the Mayor's Parlour with the Mayor, Cllr Jim Leadbeater, and Lord Aylesford, Lord Lieutenant in 1977. (*D.F. Vodden Collection*)

Wilf Sims retired in March 1975 after forty-nine years in journalism. Mr G.R. Pritchard, MD of West Midlands Press Ltd, presents retirement cheques to Mr Wilf Sims, Deputy Editor (left), having joined the *Observer* in 1951, and Mr George Wood, Head Reader since 1958. At the rear, from the left, are: Mr M.C. Adam, Financial Director, Mr D.M. Griffiths, Production Director, Mr D. Goggin, Editorial Director, Mr J. Hill, Advertisement Director, and Mr B. Dawson, Group Deputy Editor-in-Chief. Wilf Sims died soon after his wife's death on 18 November 1977, aged 67. (*Courtesy* Walsall Observer/*Craig Winyard*/*Stuart Williams*)

Mrs Edith Felgate retired in July 1980 after twenty-six years teaching about the leather industry at Walsall Art College. She is seen here receiving a gift from Deputy Principal Mr Angus Macauley. (*B. Felgate Collection*)

7

Ever-changing Townscape

The future site for Safeways in the 1990s, from the Area Health
Authority office in Lichfield Street. (*D.F. Vodden*)

Re-roofing the tower at Hydesville Tower School after the severe gale of 1990. It is this distinctive architectural feature which is part of the name of the school. More information is included in the author's history of the first fifty years of the school available from bookshops or the school. (*T.D. Farrell*)

In the late twentieth century The Bridge is now pedestrianised as the Civic Square and furnished with the Source of Ingenuity fountain by Tom Lomax. (*D.F. Vodden*)

Lower Park Street in the 1990s demonstrates the major change brought by pedestrianisation. Lloyds TSB Bank remains a landmark building on the corner. (*D.F. Vodden*)

The Shrubbery at the corner of Prince's Avenue and The Crescent, 1980. It had been the Wheways' family home. In the last couple of years it has been converted into four apartments and the former garden is now built upon to provide a further sixty-two apartments. (*R.A. Brevitt*)

The main house at The Shrubbery was converted in 2003 into four large apartments which were marketed at £250,000 each. (*D.F. Vodden*)

The main entrance to the private estate of over sixty houses on the site of the former Crabtrees' Lincoln Works, called Crabtree Road, 2000. (*D.F. Vodden*)

Following the demolition of Sainsbury's store in High Street, the site was cleared in 2005 for a new Asda, in conjunction with the development of Shannons as a shopping mall. (*D.F. Vodden*)

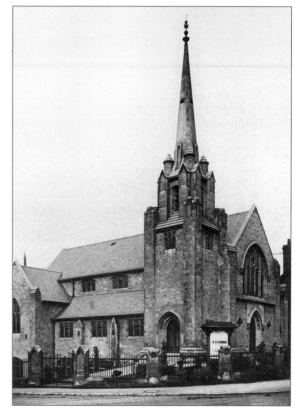

Mellish Road Methodist church, 2000. Although a Grade II listed building, it has been neglected for the past ten years; there is currently a campaign to persuade the owners to put it into a safe condition. (*D.F. Vodden*)

Mellish Road Methodist church contained this plaque commemorating its original foundation in 1909 and is seen here in 2000. The foundation stone was laid on 16 September 1909 and the church was opened on 24 May 1910, Empire Day. (*D.F. Vodden*)

The Technical College now known as WALCAT was originally built in the 1960s to the plans of R.G. Madeley FRIBA. It is now facing demolition within two or three years, once a new college is built to the north at Littleton Street. This town-centre part of the site will then become a large Tesco store. (*D.F. Vodden*)

The fairly recently built Woolworths stands at the top of Park Street, seen here in 2006. It had replaced the popular Savoy Cinema and, according to the Regeneration Company, may be demolished to open up Park Street for a Midland Metro Tramway station and the impending developments in Wolverhampton Street. (*D.F. Vodden*)

Darwall Street in May 2005, before work began pedestrianising it as part of the new Civic Quarter. (*D.F. Vodden*)

Tower Street has been altered to fit in with the new Civic Quarter scheme in 2006, with restricted vehicle access to the Gala Baths. (*D.F. Vodden*)